*Freher's Process
in the
Philosophical Work*

By
Dionysius Andreas Freher

Copyright © 2021 Lamp of Trismegistus. All rights reserved. No part of this publication may be reproduced or transmitted in any form or by any means, electronic or mechanical, including photocopying, recording, or by any information storage and retrieval system, without permission in writing from Lamp of Trismegistus. Reviewers may quote brief passages.

ISBN: 978-1-63118-514-4

*Esoteric Classics:
Studies in Alchemy*

Other Books in this Series and Related Titles

Aurora of the Philosophers by Paracelsus (978-1-63118-507-6)

Rosicrucian Rules, Secret Signs, Codes and Symbols by various (978-1-63118-488-8)

On the Philadelphian Gold by Philochrysus & Philadelphus (978-1-63118-511-3)

Paracelsus, the Four Elements and Their Spirits by M P Hall (978-1-63118-400-0)

The Stone of the Philosophers by A E Waite (978-1-63118-509-0)

The Rosicrucian Chemical Marriage by Christian Rosenkreuz (978-1-63118-458-1)

Alchemy in the Nineteenth Century by Helena P Blavatsky (978-1-63118-446-8)

The Magician's Heavenly Chaos by Thomas Vaughan (978-1-63118-500-7)

The Alchemical Catechism of Paracelsus by Paracelsus (978-1-63118-513-7)

Rosicrucians and Speculative Masonry in the Seventeenth Century (978-1-63118-489-5)

Qabbalistic Teachings and the Tree of Life by M P Hall (978-1-63118-482-6)

The Sepher Yetzirah and the Qabalah by M P Hall (978-1-63118-481-9)

The Devil in Love by Jacques Cazotte (978–1–63118–499–4)

Fortune-Telling with Dice by Astra Cielo (978-1-63118-466-6)

History, Analysis and Secret Tradition of the Tarot by Hall &c (978-1-63118-445-1)

Crystal Vision Through Crystal Gazing by Frater Achad (978-1-63118-455-0)

The Golden Verses of Pythagoras: Five Translations (978-1-63118-479-6)

Arcane Formulas or Mental Alchemy by W W Atkinson (978-1-63118-459-8)

The Machinery of the Mind by Dion Fortune (978-1-63118-451-2)

The A E Waite Reader: A Selection of Occult Essays (978-1-63118-515-1)

The Leadbeater Reader: A Selection of Occult Essays (978-1-63118-483-3)

Audio versions are also available on Audible, Amazon and Apple

Other Books in this Series and Related Titles

On the Cave of the Nymphs in the Odyssey by Thomas Taylor (978-1-63118-505-2)

The Influence of Pythagoras on Freemasonry and Other Essays (978-1-63118-404-8)

Brothers & Builders by Joseph Fort Newton (978-1-63118-506-9)

The Kabbalah of Masonry & Related Writings by E Levi &c (978-1-63118-453-6)

A Collection of Fiction and Essays by Occult Writers on Supernatural and Metaphysical Subjects by various (978–1–63118–510–6)

Cloud Upon the Sanctuary by Waite & K Eckartshausen (978-1-63118-438-3)

The Hymns of Hermes by G. R. S. Mead (978-1-63118-405-5)

The Secrets of Enoch by Enoch (978-1-63118-449-9)

Magical Essays and Instructions by Florence Farr (978-1-63118-418-5)

Masonic and Rosicrucian History by M P Hall & H Voorhis (978-1-63118-486-4)

The Sword of Welleran and Other Stories by Lord Dunsany (978-1-63118-501-4)

The Janeites, The Man Who Would Be King and Other Stories of Freemasonry by Rudyard Kipling (978–1–63118–480–2)

Gnosis of the Mind by G. R. S. Mead (978-1-63118-408-6)

The First and Second Gospels of the Infancy of Jesus Christ by Thomas and James (978-1-63118-415-4)

The Life of Pythagoras by Porphyry (978-1-63118-512-0)

Clairvoyance and Psychic Abilities by A Besant &c (978-1-63118-403-1)

Freemasonry & Catholicism by Max Heindel (978-1-63118-508-3)

The Feminine Occult by various authors (978-1-63118-711-7)

The Path of Light: A Manual of Maha-Yana Buddhism (978-1-63118-471-0)

Tao Te Ching & Commentary by Lao Tzu & C Johnston (978-1-63118-495-6)

Audio versions are also available on Audible, Amazon and Apple

Table of Contents

Introduction

Page 7

The Process in the Philosophical Work

Page 9

INTRODUCTION

The word "esoteric" can be difficult to define. Esotericism in general can be seen less as a system of beliefs and more as a category, which encompasses numerous, different systems of beliefs. It's a bit of juxtaposition, since the word "esoteric" indicates something that few people know about, while the term itself broadly covers numerous philosophies, practices, areas of study and belief systems.

In a greater sense, Esotericism acts as a storehouse for secret knowledge, which is often considered ancient *(by tradition, if not by fact),* passed down from generation to generation, in private. At various times in history, simply possessing the knowledge of some of these subjects, was considered illegal and a jailable offence, if discovered. This usually included such general topics as Alchemy, Pharmacology, Qabalah, Hermeticism, Occultism, Ceremonial Magic, Astrology, Divination, Rosicrucianism and so on. Collectively, these areas of study were often referred to as the esoteric sciences.

Sometimes, the outer garment of a subject isn't esoteric, while what is hidden beneath it, is. As an example, Freemasonry isn't necessarily esoteric by nature (at *least not anymore),* but certain signs, passwords and handshakes given to the candidate during their initiation, are in fact, esoteric, in the sense that they are hidden from the general public.

Today, in the twenty-first century, such topics are readily available at bookstores across the country, and numerous mainsteam publishers offer beginners guides and coffee-table volumes on many of these subjects, intended for mass appeal. Books like *"The Secret"* have turned previously arcane topics into household knowledge. All that being the case, however, it isn't to say that there still aren't buried secrets to uncover, ancient wisdom being ignored and forgotten mysteries to be explored. In fact, it is often that we are only able to further our own studies by standing on the shoulders of these disappearing giants.

Lamp of Trismegistus is doing its part to help preserve humanity's esoteric history by making some of these classics available to those students who are seeking to unearth the knowledge of these ancient colossi.

So, be sure to check other titles from our *Esoteric Classics* series, as well as our *Occult Fiction, Theosophical Classics, Foundations of Freemasonry Series, Supernatural Fiction, Paranormal Research Series, Studies in Buddhism* and our *Christian Apocrypha Series.* You can also download the audio versions of most of these titles from Amazon, Apple or Audible, for learning on the go.

THE PROCESS IN THE PHILOSOPHICAL WORK CONSIDERED AS THOROUGHLY ANALOGICAL WITH THAT IN MAN'S REDEMPTION THROUGH JESUS CHRIST AND REPRESENTED BY POSITIONS GIVEN THEREOF, AS TO ITS PRINCIPAL POINTS IN BEHMEN'S *SIGNATURA RERUM*, CHAPTERS VII, X, XI and XII

1. Adam's primeval state in Paradise, and the manner of his spoiling himself, his whole created being, by his lustful imagination after the knowledge of good and evil, is rightly by this author, not only spoken of in the first beginning of his description, but also frequently repeated and variously expressed throughout his whole discourse. For if Man understandeth not his own corrupted nature, and that curse which he himself lieth under, how can he be imagined to be able for an understanding of the nature and curse of the Earth? Or upon what ground can he presume to deliver such or such a particular thing from that curse; or to be instrumental in this deliverance? which is the true Artist's chiefest, nay only business.

2. As long as Adam stood in a pure paradisical innocency, the Eternal Word and power of life (called by the author the Heavenly Mercury), was his leader, and had pre-dominance in him. His life, which was a clear flaming fire, burned in and was nourished by that pure spiritual oil of the Divine substantiality; which, together with the holy water of eternal life, is generated in the angelical world: and this, therefore, could not but give forth a glorious bright shining light.

3. Through the power of his imagination, or lust after the knowledge of good and evil, that which then was still kept under in him, and was so hidden from him, viz., the outward watery property, came to be manifest in his holy oil, and got predominance therein. This oil therefore, now overpowered thereby, could no more be such an agreeable food, and well-doing to his fire, as it could and did before. And so his fire not only lost its shining light, but came also to be spoiled itself, for it was obscured, and made all impotent. And his Mercury, which before in his holy oil, had caused and raised up paradisical joy and triumph, according to his moving and stirring property, was now made a stinging anguishing poison, according to his own natural constitution, which he doth and must stand in, when before or without the light.

4. Nothing of the Divine substantiality was hereby spoiled, poisoned, or turned into evil: though sometimes this or that expression, which must be made use of with respect to Man, may seem in outward appearance, to say something the like. For that which was in Man of the Divine substantiality, faded disappeared, or died indeed, but only with respect to Man; seeing that this disappearing, was but an entering into its own secret original, and so but a returning unto God the giver thereof. When contrariwise the creatural Mercury, that is, Man's own life, went forth with its will, desire and lust, out of eternity into time: so that the former union was broken, and upon this breach, its own natural property and propriety could not but be made manifest immediately: and because of this manifestation, which never should have been made, according to the will of God, it is now rightly called spoiled, poisoned, and turned into evil; when yet all this doth not reach the Divine substantiality, nor the holy life of God, but only that of Man.

5. This is the sum and substance of what Behmen largely and more circumstantially declareth concerning Man's paradisical state, and falling away from it under the curse. Where he brings in also for a clearer illustration hereof, not only the fall of Lucifer, saying of him, that his desire was to try the fiery Mercury, like as Man desired to try the watery; but also the serpent with its poison, saying, that in the strongest and most poisonous Mercury, the highest tincture lieth, yet not in its own natural property, etc. All which he represents as a most proper, and pertinent introduction to this discourse of the Philosophical Work.

6. Immediately after the fall of Man, God said unto the serpent, I will put enmity between thee and the woman, and between thy seed and her seed: her seed shall bruise thy head, and thou shalt bruise his heel. And herein the philosopher's stone or tincture lieth implicitly. For though this primarily concerneth Man, yet secondarily it concerneth the whole Creation also; and this bruising of the serpent's head is done both spiritually and corporeally, and both in time and in eternity, and though in different degrees, yet in a parallel process or method, both here and there.

7. The serpent's sting points at the Wrath-fire, and the woman's seed at the Light and Love-fire. These two are in every thing: and in the curse that former came to be predominant in outward Nature. This latter must now be raised up again, and, by its shining through the Wrath, it must subdue and keep it under, and take away from it its predominant power, so that it may keep and exercise only its true natural office, as a servant in and to the light. And that these two may no more stand in contrariety and opposition to each other, but be one only thing, reharmonized by Light and Love, and reintroduced into Paradise. And when now thus the dark poisoned Mercury is tinctured, his anguishing death is turned into triumphing life and joy, and his former dark desire into a new Light and Love-desire; which of itself is now able to make in itself a pure Love and Light substantiality, viz., a heavenly body out of an earthly.

8. The whole work consists summarily therein, that two things must be reduced back into one, even into such a one as they were from the beginning before they came to be two. A heavenly thing and an earthly one are to be joined. That former must be admitted or received into itself by this latter, and must change it into its own heavenly quality. Earth must be turned in, and Heaven out, etc. Which the Mercury, that is therein, doth all himself; the Artist is not to do it, neither can he do it: he is only to join together those ingredients that are requisite, and to leave the work to be done by that workman, which is therein already. Yet nevertheless Understanding and Faith is in him required; and by this latter especially he is to co-operate, if his design shall take effect. For his design is nothing less than to fetch out a body from the curse, and to raise it up from the dead; which never can be done by him, that is still dead himself, both in his understanding, and as to his internal life.

9. With all this, the process in the regeneration of Man runs parallel exactly. Consider only with thyself the heavenly humanity of the Regenerator, and the earthly of poor fallen Man, that is to be regenerated. Consider, that the former must be received or taken in by the latter, and that this must suffer itself to be subdued, changed, kept under, and turned in by that. Consider that faith in Man is absolutely required, by which he must in a sense co-operate indeed, but that for all this he cannot make himself a Child of God; but must suffer himself to be made so by the eternal speaking Word, which in the philosophical process is called by Behmen, the Heavenly Mercury. Which also at the end of time, as in the completest period of the regeneration, will raise up his body again, which then shall no more be earthly, but heavenly, and conformable to his own glorified body. Consider, I say, all this in its true coherence, and dependence upon the only love and free grace of God: and you will certainly find, that all the description of this process, is nothing else but a sound, true and solid paraphrase and explanation of these words of

St. John, saying: "As many as received him, to them gave he power to become the Sons of God, even to them that believe in his name."

10. In these words also lieth plainly, the possibility for obtaining the perfection in the Philosophical Work; which is rightly and firmly grounded hereupon by Behmen. For if God gave us, out of his infinite love, that which is the greatest and the highest, how could he have withheld from us, that which is much lesser and lower? If Man, in this divine power, bestowed upon him by free grace, can verily rule and triumph again over sin, death, devil, and hell, whom he made himself subject unto by his lust, Why should he not also be enabled thereby, to rule and triumph again over the curse in the Earth, he brought into it by the same lust, when this latter is but a natural consequence of that former; nay an inconsiderable one in comparison to that? Truly it is inseparable therefrom, if that former be really attained unto, and provided that all the qualities that are requisite thereto, be verily found in the Artist or philosopher.

11. All these qualities are, as in their principal sum and substance, concentrated in this, that the Artist first must have the curse in himself transmuted into the Heavenly Blessing, through the holy tincturing blood of Jesus Christ. Which Behmen sometimes also thus expresses, "He must first be, and have really that same in himself, which he will make or introduce into metals without himself". And this he frequently presseth home unto every one, warning earnestly and calling Heaven and Earth to witnesses, that none shall presume to meddle with the curse in the Earth, before he be really delivered, as to his inward Man, from that curse in himself; or else he may expect to earn nothing else but curse instead of blessing. Before this his own internal deliverance, he may have indeed so many fine notions of this work in his brain; but the real process cannot be manifest in him, and so not understood by him, in that experimental fullness and exactness which is required.

12. The same he offers also to the serious consideration of such a one, under these and the like philosophical terms - He is to know that his Mercury is kindled in the fiery Mars, and burns in the eternal Saturn, in the terrible impression of darkness; his Venus is captivated, his water dried up, his Jupiter is become a fool, his Sun is darkened, and his Moon turned into a black night. And now there is no other remedy but to take Venus (the eternal love of God) and to introduce that into his poisoned Mercury and Mars, that they may be tinctured thereby, and then his Sun will shine again and Jupiter rejoice, etc. Which he further illustrates, by plain intelligible words, all representing most excellently his own way, practice and experience.

13. Yet all this, though really attained unto, will not be yet fully sufficient. For there is not only such a sufficient ability for this work, and a sufficient understanding of its process required, which I doubt not but Behmen had; but there is also required an especial calling thereunto, which he had not. Without this calling the Artist goes but in his own will; though his meaning and intent, as to his thinking were never so good and pure. And this call he must be able to discern, by his own internal character, which it carrieth along with and in itself, from his own natural impulse. Which easily may delude him, under the specious appearance of a divine call; and whereby the spirit of this world, which from its own internal constitution, is mightily for such an undertaking, will certainly mislead him into various dangers.

14. When now these two more general requisites viz., (1) An experimental understanding, from the Artist's process in his own regeneration, and (2) a divine call for this understanding, are truly found in him, two other more particular qualities will still be required in him, when he now is to make a beginning of his work. And these are represented by Behmen from that parable of our

Lord, concerning a man which went down from Jerusalem to Jericho, and was robbed and wounded by highwaymen. Saying, "That the Artist must truly and wholly stand in the figure of the merciful Samaritan and must have both his will and eyes." His will, that he may desire nothing else, but to heal and restore that which is wounded and broken. And his eyes, that he may be able to discern that wounded body which he is to heal, and which is not easily to be discerned, and not by every one, because of its great corruption.

15. These eyes he shall have the greatest need of in his very first beginning, when he is to choose the proper matter for this Philosophical Work. This is called by Behmen and described parabolically - "That evil child, which is run from its mother's house (from Jerusalem to Jericho) and desired to be in self, or to stand by itself upon its own bottom". And this must be sought for in Saturn; which Saturn therefore, the Artist must have sharp and piercing eyes to look into, both as to eternal and temporal nature. For the Wrath of God, by its strong astringent impression (says he further) hath shut it up into the chamber of death. Not hath it turned the same into Saturn. [Which I think is to say so much, as that it is not turned into lead.], but it keeps it imprisoned in the Saturnish death, in the first cold, hard, dark, astringent Property; which is called the great still standing death, because as yet there is no mobility of life therein.

16. When this proper matter is found in Saturn, the Artist may go to work, but so, that he do consider and follow that same process, which God observed in the redemption and restoration of mankind through Jesus Christ, (in which twofold holy Name, the general process was clearly understood by Behmen from the language of Nature), even from his conception and nativity, unto his Resurrection and Ascension. So doing, he may come to find the joyful feast of Pentecost, viz., that desirable tincture in outward Nature, which is answering unto that holy spiritual tincture, whereby

St Peter, in his first public sermon, on the day of Pentecost, tinctured three thousand souls at once.

17. When the human Mercury, the outspoken word of the human life, was infected and poisoned by the serpent, or manifest and predominant in its own natural quality, which it hath in itself, before and without the Light, God did not reject the humanity, so as to annihilate it wholly, and to make another new, and strange Adam, but he restored or regenerated that which thus was spoiled. And this he effected not by any such new or strange thing, as which the humanity had not had in it before; but by that self-same holy divine Mercury, which was at first breathed into Adam, for to make him an image and likeness of God. This he re-introduced into the poisoned humanity, and made thereby a good, sure and solid disposition to the new regeneration thereof. And this was done in the immaculate conception of Jesus Christ. For therein conjunction was made, between the eternal speaking, and the human outspoken Word, Mercury, or human life, now poisoned in Man, and full of self or own will.

18. This must be the first consideration of the Artist, well to be observed, that so he may be sure to act accordingly, and to bring not his subject matter to the fire, without such a previous conjunction; if he will not work in vain, and make himself ridiculous. And for an illustration hereof this may serve: in the Second Principle, of Light, the Love-desire, that is, the first property of Eternal Nature, but considered as in the fifth, makes a pure crystalline substantiality. And therein the divine Mercury is the eternal holy Word and understanding: but in the first principle, wherein the harsh astringent desire makes a dark obscure substantiality, the same Mercury is a principal part, or chief property of the Wrath of God, and an original of all mobility, and moving power. This Mercury therefore (considered as in the outspoken

Word, or life of Man) after it was turned away from the second principle, of Love and Light, and was made manifest according to its own wrathful property in the first; could not have been restored or brought back again, but by that very same Mercury, which was first breathed into Man, and was not altered in the Light and Love of God, though it was altered in Man, in whom it disappeared and lost its former pre-dominion. Now the getting this lost pre-dominion again, either in Man, or in any other creature, according to its own kind, is nothing else, but that same tincturing and transmuting, which in all this discourse is spoken of; and which restored pre-dominion therefore of that Heavenly Mercury must needs reproduce again such a pure light's substantiality, as that which disappeared in Man, by his fall, and in the Earth by the curse.

19. In the relation of St. Luke, concerning what the child Jesus did with his parents, in the twelfth year of his age, a representation is seen of the inward and outward world, and of their different wills. For the inward will in Jesus broke first the natural will of his parents, when he remained in the temple, without their knowing and consent, nay said also, like as rebuking them, "How is it that ye sought me? Wist ye not that I must be about my Father's business?" And then again, the will of this outward world in his parents, broke the inward will in Jesus, for he went down with them to Nazareth, and was subject unto them. This showeth to the Artist, that in his work he shall soon find such a two-fold will also. The will of the inward world, will not in the beginning presently condescend and be subject to his will. But if he ceaseth not to seek after it, as Mary did, and wrestleth with it all the night like Jacob, with a full resignation of his own will, which is the will of this outward world, this divine Will, will at length condescend to him, and go down with him; for it is as it were broken or conquered by his will, according to what was said to Jacob: thou has wrestled with God and Man and hast prevailed.

20. Here the Artist, or magus is to know, that he is not to bring that will or tendency to the perfection, into his Matter from without, but that it lieth therein already before. He must only first in himself be capable of the Divine Will, and then with his renewed, or tinctured will, which here is his magical faith, he must handle his subject matter; that so thereby the will towards perfection, which lieth in the matter indeed, but still and unmoveable, may be stirred up and brought into conjunction with his human tinctured will, and so also with the Divine Will. And that further this Divine Will may press forward or outwards, meet with and bless that outward will, which presseth backwards or inwards from the corruption into God's Love and mercy.

21. Highly is this point unto the Artist recommended, not only for to consider and understand, but also to make it his continual practice. Because herein the Philosophical Baptism, as to the greatest or chiefest deal consisteth, and this practice is the very first beginning thereof. This only can make him able to baptize truly and rightly, for he is to baptize his matter, not only with the water of the outward, but also with that of the inward world. Of which baptism more must be said now by and by.

22. The poor fallen humanity, considered so barely as it was in and to itself, viz., as broken, spoiled, poisoned, was not cast immediately into the fiery furnace, and melted down by the Wrath of God; but, as mentioned above, a conjunction was first made between the Earthly and Heavenly humanity. Neither came the great fiery trial upon it, immediately after this conjunction; but a long and wonderful process was held, before it came to that great earnest. First, the humanity was to be baptized with water in the Jordan, and with water from above the firmament. Further it was led into the wilderness, for to be tempted by the Devil, which devil (N.B.) was not put into the humanity, but permitted to stand over against it, and to offer unto it all that the first Adam was tempted with. And all this time of forty days, no outward food was given to this new baptized humanity, but it was to live upon its own life's Mercurius, viz., the Eternal Word proceeding from the mouth of God, according to the answer the Lord Jesus gave unto the Devil. After this he came forth in public, preached, and did great wonders and miracles in all the seven Properties of Nature. And though at length even his human body was really glorified upon the Holy Mount, and seen so by three of his disciples, yet by all this, the full perfection was not yet wrought out, but the very greatest, sharpest and most severe trial was still behind, etc. Answerably to all this process, the Philosophical Work also must be carried on, and the Artist will see a continual parallelism; but at length he will find also, that all this, though it was shown him in never so glorious an appearance, is still short of perfection, and all but as it were preliminary, which now further distinctly shall appear.

23. By the Philosophical Baptism, if it be truly performed, in the dead Mercury, which lieth in impotence, and hungers only after its own Property, being of itself not capable, either of desiring after, or of admitting into it any other, the hunger after the divine or heavenly substantiality is stirred and raised up again. And by this hunger, that heavenly substantiality is drawn in, with its own peculiar will, desire, or natural inclination, which is nothing else but a readiness, or tendency to become manifest with its life in the death. And herein is the first beginning of a new body, or rather of a seed, from which a new body is to come forth in its due time.

24. What this Philosophical Baptism is, and the absolute necessity thereof, may thus be shortly represented: Every hunger is a desire after such a thing as is agreeable and conformable to that hunger: for after that which is disagreeing and contrary, or destructive to it, no hunger in anything can be. The dead corrupted

Mercury then hath a hunger indeed, but only (according to its condition in the Curse), after death, wrath and poison, etc. If now to this hunger such a dead and wrathful thing is given, as it hungers after, the death therein must needs increase, and its wrathfulness cannot but be strengthened thereby. But if to this hunger the life is presented, or a loving, heavenly property is offered, the death is not at all able to receive it. Unto this death therefore, the death and Wrath of God must be given, but in this death and Wrath the heavenly substantiality. And this is the Philosophical Baptism, for this is that Earthly and Heavenly water, in the first of which is death, and in the second life: both which must be together; for the reason is now plain, why neither by this nor by that alone, this baptism can be performed. But when it is thus rightly done, this baptism, viz., that which is heavenly swalloweth up into death that which is earthly and wrathful, and exalts its own new life therein; though not immediately, like as it was also not done in Christ immediately after his baptism.

25. This Philosophical Baptism is nothing else but a conjunction, to be made between the fiery and watery Mercury. The fiery must be baptized with the watery. And this is what Behmen means by saying obscurely: "Have a care only for this, that thou baptisest the mercury with his own baptism." For this watery Mercury is his own, viz., it is that, which before the Fall and Curse he enjoyed and rejoiced in, as his most precious treasure; whereby his fiery poisonous Wrath, was kept under, and prevented from being manifest. But when these two were separated from each other, a breach was made, which cannot be healed again, but by a renewed conjunction between them. Like as it is in animals and in fallen Man also the same thing, only in different in degrees. The conjunction of male and female, which is absolutely required, to the multiplication of every kind of living creatures (which hath in vegetables also something answering thereunto), may be a good illustration thereof.

26. And therefore it is that by Behmen this very same, which here now is called the Philosophical Baptism, is called also and compared to a matrimony or espousal, when he plainly says, not only that to the Earthly wrathful Mercury, a fair loving virgin of his own kind must be given in marriage; but also that this same giving is the Philosophical Baptism. And again says he, "The woman's (not the man's) seed shall bruise the serpent's head." The man hath in his tincture the fire-spirit, and the woman in hers the water-spirit. This latter must baptize, soften, appease and overcome that former, and so transmute its strong fiery hunger after Wrath, into a tender Love-desire; and herein lieth the baptism of Nature. In this steadfast Love-desire, these two are at last turned into one, so that they are not more male and female, fire and water in contrariety, but a masculine virgin with both tinctures in union. But before this be wholly effected, and as long as they are in the way or process thereunto, Behmen calleth them in all this discourse, the young man and the virgin, or also the Bridegroom and the Bride.

27. Immediately after the baptism of Christ, he was led by the Spirit into the wilderness, to be tempted by the devil. And a serious consideration of the whole process in this threefold temptation, is highly unto the Artist recommended; for in his Philosophical Work the same must be done also, in a total answerableness to the three particulars therein, relating to the three first properties. All which is largely by Behmen declared, and much insisted upon, but would be too long for to relate particularly. Yet the sum and substance thereof is this:-

28. The human Soul, or the whole humanity as an image of the eternal speaking Word, was now tried, after God had re-introduced into it a spark of his Eternal Love, whether it would enter again into its primeval state and place and be an instrument of God, to be played upon by his holy Spirit, in his Love; or whether it would rather continue in its own will, and suffer the Devil to play upon its instrument in the Wrath and Anger of God. And so in the Philosophical Work also, the earthly poisonous Mercury, after he is now joined again to the heavenly, is tried, whether he will go out from his own natural wrathful property, and suffer himself to be turned into his first, pure and crystalline condition, wherein he stood before the curse: or whether he will rather continue in his own awakened and now predominant quality.

29. In our Lord Jesus Christ, the human will rejected all the devil's presentations and offerings, resigned itself, and entered wholly into the first mother's womb, according to his words to Nicodemus, etc. And so in the Philosophical Work, if it goes well and right the Artist will see, that when the tempter comes on, the young man, or Mercury gives himself up wholly into the first Mother, and that this will swallow him up as into nothing. At which the Artist will be amazed and terrified, thinking that all is lost and undone, for he sees nothing, and hath lost all the appearance of heaven. But he must have patience, that which is impossible in his sight, is not so in the powers of Nature.

30. The wilderness wherein the temptation is done, is, in this Philosophical Work, the outward, earthly, dry, desolate and barren body. Wherein the Mercury or young man, is not able to stand against the devil, except he lay hold on his virgin, and be by her supported. He is therefore to unite with her, to cast his will and desire into her love, and to eat of her bread, not of his own natural quality, like as Christ our Lord, all the forty days of his temptation, did eat only of the eternal speaking Word, and would not eat of that bread, which he could have made out of the stones. All which is nothing else but that the Mercury must admit and receive into its own poisonous quality, the Heavenly Tincture, and suffer the serpent's head, the fiery wrathful property, to be bruised thereby in himself. Which if doth not, the Devil will prevail, and detain him captive in that state, wherein he is when separated from his Virgin. But if he doth the Devil must withdraw, and the Virgin takes his seed from him into her womb.

31. What the Devil is in this work, the Artist, says Behmen, will easily know, but he calls him not by any plain or distinct name: doubtless it is such another wrathful dark and poisonous matter, as may be fitly compared to the devil, and may be able to do in this process, the devil's office, because of the qualities alike in both. For this will appear afterwards, as to my thinking, plainly enough, and here also it may be seen in part, from that instruction and warning, he gives to the Artist, viz., He shall have a care, to suffer not. Thus, says he, he shall have a care, to suffer not, that his tempting devil be too furious, or too wrathful, but proportionable, etc. And again, on the other hand, that he be not too weak or impotent, for else the Mercury should not be assaulted by him sufficiently, and might as a hungry wolf, swallow up his baptism, return to his own wrathful property, and continue still that same poisonous thing, which he was before.

32. At the end of forty days, when the Devil had ended all the temptation, he must depart from the Lord Christ, and the angels came and ministered unto him. This also the Artist is especially well to observe, for he himself stood here in the trial also, and may now perceive infallibly, whether or no, he be fit for, and accounted worthy of this work. If at the end of forty days, in answerableness to the process of Christ, the angels do not appear, he may surely think of himself, that he is not yet fit and worthy; and of his fiery masculine Mercury, that this doth not yet stand in a due internal union with the watery feminine, but that it is still that same, in its own wrathful quality, which it was before, and that the tempting devil hath prevailed. But if he seeth the sign of the Angels, he may rejoice and be sure, that the Bridegroom is in his Bride, and she in him, and that his work can prosper. What this sign of the angels is, the author doth not tell us expressly; it must be some new delightful appearance, by its own character so intelligible to the Artist, as that was intelligible to him, when before he saw nothing, and had lost the appearance of heaven.

33. Immediately after this temptation, and overcoming of the devil, the Lord Christ began his public office, not only by preaching, reproving and instructing the people, but also, by working many great miraculous, amazing things, through all the Properties of Nature. For instance: in Saturn, he raised up the dead; in Luna, he transmuted water into wine, and fed with five loaves of bread five thousand men; in Jupiter, he made out of the simple and ignorant fishermen, the most wise and understanding apostles. In Mercury, he made the deaf hearing, the dumb speaking, and healed the lepers. In Mars he expelled devils from the possessed. In Venus, he loved his brethren and sisters, as to the humanity, and gave freely his life for them into death. Only six of the properties are here enumerated, and the seventh which is Sol, standing in the midst and uniting three and three, is here not mentioned, because this belongeth to the full perfection, which then only was attained unto, when he was risen from the dead, ascended up to heaven, and had poured out the holy Tincturing Spirit, on the day of Pentecost. But that there is a good ground for Behmen's referring distinctly to the seven Properties of Nature, all the miraculous deeds of Christ, could be made out from him sufficiently, were it needful and not too large.

34. All this now the Artist shall distinctly see, that it hath a true and exact answerableness in the Philosophical Work, when the forty days temptation with good success is ended. For instance, in Saturn, he shall see, that now the Mercury raiseth up from death that same dead substance, wherein he was shut up before. In Luna, that he feedeth and nourisheth that substance, when there is nothing outwardly wrought, which it could be fed and nourished with: and again, that the deadly water is exalted and turned into wine, by having now got (like as wine hath) an union of a fiery and watery virtue. In Jupiter, he shall see the four elements each by itself, and their colours, and the rainbow upon which Christ sitteth for judgment, in the outspoken Mercury. So that he highly shall be amazed at it, and perceive that the wisdom of God playeth and delighteth therein as in a jestful play. For the friendly Jupiter showeth forth herein his properties, after such a manner as that is, in which God will, in its time change this world and transmute it into Paradise. In Mercury, he shall see that Heaven separates itself from the Earth, and that it sinks down again into the Earth, and changeth the same into its own colour, and that Mercurypurifieth the matter, etc. In Mars, he shall see, that Jupiter in the Mercury, casts out from the matter upwards a black fire smoke, which will be coagulated like as a soot in the chimney. And this is the poisonous hunger in the Mercury, rightly to be compared to the devil, because it hath, according to its own kind, the devil's qualities. What Christ did in Venus, the Artist shall see most gloriously in the Philosophical Work. For as soon as this black devil is expelled from the matter, Venus in her virginity appears, in great beauty and glory, which is a fine type or emblem of the great love of Christ.

35. Now here, when this appears, the Artist is rejoiced, and thinks reasonably his work is finished, and he hath got the treasure of the World; but soon shall he find himself extremely disappointed. For when he trieth it, he shall find, it is but Venus, still a female, and not yet a pure and perfect virgin, with both tinctures united into one. Like as in Christ, the Eternal speaking Word had indeed wrought out through his humanity, all these wondrous deeds; and yet the full perfection could not be made manifest therein, his human body could not be glorified, and much less could he have poured out the

Holy Ghost, before he was passed through the great Anger of God or Death and Hell. So also in this Philosophical Work, though all these glorious things have appeared in the Properties of Nature, yet the universal Tincture is not yet fixed and manifest, but all what was seen hitherto, was only transient, and the greatest work to be done, for this fixation and manifestation, is still behind. For all the seven Properties must be made totally pure and crystalline, before they can be Paradisical, and each of them hath its own peculiar process, when it is to go out from the wrathful into the Paradisical life; wherein they must all seven have but one will, viz., that of Love, and all their former own will, wherein each was for itself, in opposition to the others, must be utterly swallowed up. And then only they are fixed, and able to abide the fire, for then no Turba can be more therein. Which is now further effected by a process answering to that which was observed in the suffering and death of Christ.

36. As soon as the regenerator of mankind came into this World from above, and had the name of a king given unto him, the civil government thereof could not endure him; but presently he was by Herod persecuted, and at length by Pilate crucified, notwithstanding that he had plainly declared that his kingdom was not of this world. And because this newborn king came not not with a royal state and splendour, nor in such an outward power, as the Jews expected and hoped for, at the coming of their Messiah, the Ecclesiastical government in the high priest and Pharisees, would not receive him. And since he owned himself to be the Son of God, and a king of truth, and said he was come to save his people from their sins and darkness, and from the Wrath to come, the Devil also could not endure him; but he was immediately a strong opposition against these three together in conjunction. So also in this Philosophical Work, as soon as Venus thus appears in her beauty, with her own natural character, and in order to perfection, there is a great alarm, opposition and insurrection against her, manifest in

Saturn, Mercury and Mars. The first of which is a true figure of the civil government, the second of the Ecclesiastical state, and the third of the Devil. And as these three jointly were the same chief agents, that brought the Lord of Life and Glory unto death; so in this Philosophical Work, the three inferior wrathful Properties, Saturn, Mercury and Mars, are rightly called by Behmen the three murderers of Venus.

37. This great opposition and uproar against the Lord Christ, had, in the internal truth and reality no other ground but this, that he was from above, when all these three were from beneath. Deep, great, and many things are in these few words comprised, and the essential nature of a Principle (taken in Behmen's sense) is understood therein. If the Lord had been out of their own dark, harsh, bitter and wrathful root, and if he had appeared, for to preserve and establish the same, in its own selfish and willful qualities, they would have received him very kindly, and no opposition could have been made. But he was from another Principle, and came only for to destroy the works of the Devil in this world, and to recall its inhabitants unto Light, Love and Truth. Now all this was bad news in the ears of all these three parties, for none of them was willing to be stripped of its selfish greatness, dignity, strength and power; and therefore they all three at length agreed for his crucifixion. So also in this Philosophical Work, there is no other ground for this great opposition, but this very same, that Venus is from above, when these three are from beneath; united in one wrathful sphere, and unwilling to be deprived of their natural power and pre-dominion. Heaven stands now in Hell, upon Earth, and will transmute them both into Paradise; and Hell perceiveth its ruin is inevitable, if it receives into it this child from heaven; and therefore it swelleth up against it, and opposeth all what it can. But by this same opposition, it must and doth but promote its own destruction; as it was done also in the process of Christ.

38. Here might be objected, How can all this be consistent with what was done and declared above, viz., that the matter was purified, the devil expelled, and the sign of the angels appeared, etc? For if so, whence can now such a wrathful, hellish opposition arise? But it is easily to be answered, and the answer Behmen gives to it (though but implicitly and not so directly) is of the greatest importance, not only in this process of the Philosophical Work, but also especially in that of Man's Regeneration. When Mercury, (says he) is awakened from the death of Saturn's strong impression, and receiveth Manna (heavenly food, Light's and Love's substantiality, his own true Virgin, the Water of Life, the Philosophical Baptism) into the mouth of his poisonous Property, a joyful crack ariseth indeed; for it is like as if a light were kindled in the darkness, and a paradisical joy and Love springeth in the midst of Wrath. When now Mercury thus gets a twinkling glimpse thereof in Mars, the wrathfulness is terrified at the Love, and falleth back or sinketh down, like as in the generation of the second Principle out of the first; and the angelical properties appear as in a glimpse. And so this is (N.B. not yet a transmutation but) like as a transmutation, but only transient not yet constant or fixed. If therefore a fixed and radical transmutation shall be done, the same process, that was in this like a transmutation, must be repeated again; but in a far higher or rather deeper degree; And the same can also be repeated again, because the harsh, bitter, wrathful hellish Properties were hitherto suppressed only in part, but not fully rooted out, and radically turned into one only will. And they therefore are now raised afresh by this appearance of Venus, nay even much more than ever before, they stand up in opposition against her, for to maintain their own natural right. So that here also, in a sense, the words of Christ are true, saying I am come to kindle a fire, and to bring upon Earth a sword, enmity, strife, persecution, war and opposition.

39. This opposition is, in this Philosophical Work, between three and three; like as it is also in the generation of Eternal Nature. Yet this is to be understood in such a sense, as the foregoing 38th position can bear, wherein there was asserted, that here nothing as yet is permanent and fixed. So it was also in the process with the Lord Christ: when he now was a going into the strong severity of the Wrath and Anger of God, in order to the full consummation of his great work, he said expressly of himself, "I am not alone, but the Father is with me." He had then with him on the one side, or as we may say, from above, the Father, and him unalterably, in one sense, though changeably in another, relating to the sensibility of his outward human person. Which may appear, by his woeful crying out on the cross, "My God, My God, why hast thou forsaken me?" For that which here by some is now objected, concerning a wrong translation of these words, is not to be regarded, because the sense wherein they are taken is not liable to such ill constructions and consequences as they put upon it. And on the other side, or as from beneath, he had with him, though in a very low and inconsiderable sense, the common ignorant people which received and accompanied him with great joy and acclamations, when he came riding upon an ass into Jerusalem. So also in this Philosophical Work, Venus is not alone; but, as it were, from above, Jupiter is with her, and from beneath Luna, which is a true figure of that vulgar, simple, ignorant crew. This Luna holds with Venus (like as also the Disciples themselves did with Christ), so long as it goes well with her, or at least tolerably; that is, so long as Saturn, Mercury, and Mars do not actually and manifestly exert their malice against her. But when these three murderers arise, and will forcibly put her to death, or swallow her up into their wrathful pit, then Luna also changeth her colour and inclination; like as the vulgar people changed their will, and instead of their former "Hosanna", cried now out, "Crucify, crucify him."

40. In the process of Christ, when it cometh to the Great Earnest, not only that which was done with him outwardly, by the Pharisees, High Priests, etc., but also that which was done within his own person, in Body, Soul and Spirit must be considered. The two Internal Worlds or two Eternal Principles, viz. the strong Fire-world with the properties of Wrath and anger, and the Holy Light-world, with the pure Love and Light's substantiality, or heavenly flesh and blood, were both manifest in him, and stood open the one against the other; And the great work of redemption could not have been performed, except they entered into one another essentially: for else no solid, permanent and fixed transmutation of the first into the second, could have been effected. This now made an inexpressible terror in the humanity of Christ, viz., in his whole person, considered in all the three Worlds or Principles. For the Love was struck with terror, and trembled at the rough, harsh and bitter death, which it was to give up itself into; so as to be swallowed up by the wrathful properties of anger, all now distinctly raised up and qualifying according to their own nature. And the Anger also was struck with terror, and trembled at the appearance of Love, wherein it was to lose its own wrathful and now predominant life. And so from hence the outward human body also, in this third Principle, was so violently struck with terror and trembling, that the sweat thereof was, as it were great drops of blood, falling down to the ground. Yet he said then, "Father, if it be possible, let this cup pass from me, nevertheless not my will, but thine be done." Which words are to be understood, as spoken by the whole person of Christ, viz., in each World and Property, according to the different condition of each. For the first Principle, or Anger said, "Let this cup of Love be removed from me, that I may keep my dominion in men, because of their transgression"; like as we may see an excellent type thereof in Moses, when the Wrath of God said unto him, "Let me alone, that I may devour this disobedient people." But Moses in the figure of Christ, and Christ in the highest operation of Love, would not let him, but replied, first indeed as it were to the same purpose, "If it be possible let this cup of Anger pass from me", but added also immediately, "Nevertheless not my will, but thine be done." Whereby now the human will of Christ as to this Third Principle resigned wholly and submitted itself to the will of the angry father, and was obedient unto him, even unto the death on the Cross, and unto all what was to be inflicted upon him outwardly also, by the instruments of God's Anger. So also in this Philosophical Work, when it cometh to this Great Earnest, the Artist shall plainly perceive a great terror and trembling therein; he shall see, that Mercury especially, which is the principal agent against Venus (like as the High Priests and Pharisees, were also the principal opposers and persecutors of Christ), trembleth at the appearance of Venus, and that Venus also not only trembleth at this opposition of the three wrathful murdering properties, but also that it is with her like as if a sweat did break out from her body: and that nevertheless she is not stirring, but quiet and patient, resigned and ready for to suffer all what they can inflict upon her, and to be wholly swallowed up by them into their wrathfulness.

41. In the process of Christ, the Devil said, or thought within himself, "I am alone the great monarch in the Fire, Saturn is my might, and Mercury my life, and I am in, and through them, a Prince and God of this world, and will therefore not suffer, that such another one as calls himself a Prince of Love, should rule therein, but I will devour him in my Wrath, together with his Love." This he intended indeed, but being he could not effect it as by himself alone, without concurrence of the two chief principalities of this outward world, he stirred up Mercury and Saturn, the Ecclesiastical and the Civil government. And so these all three went out together, or sent their emissaries, apprehended the Lord, bound and carried him from the one unrighteous judge to the other, etc. Thus also in the

Philosophical Work the Artist shall plainly see, that Venus, which is all passive and wholly resigned and ready to enter into the dragon's jaws, is surrounded on every side by Saturn, Mars and Mercury. And so as it were apprehended or captivated by these three in conjunction, nay also further that they lay hold on her, and bind her, by darting their several poisonous rays upon her; and then moreover, that they do, as it were, carry her from the one Property of wrathfulness to the other, like as to be by them tried, examined and judged.

42. In the first place, Mars bringeth Venus to Mercury, like as the devil's agents instruments in the Wrath of God, brought the Lord Christ first to the High Priest. But as this was already beforehand pre-possessed with hatred against him, and did not truly or duly try him, nor could look into his Internal will and work of Love, but looked upon him only from without, examined him superficially, and concluded, that since he stood not with them, in the same will, way and form, he was not to be tolerated among the living. But seeing that he could not bring in execution his design to kill him, he sent him to Pilate, with the character of an evil doer, that had deserved death. So also in this Philosophical Work, this very same is the true internal signature of Mercury, against Venus. He was before already before possessed with his own hateful quality, and stood in opposition against her, and is therefore not able to try, much less to approve of the loving Property of Venus, but hath only a will and ability to murder her. But seeing that there is in Venus another living Mercury, from above, he cannot destroy her by his own power, but must confederate himself with Saturn; and unto him he delivereth this Venus, for to be killed. Like as Christ was delivered to Pontius Pilate for to be crucified.

43. Pilate, a governor or Lord in the dark Saturnish impression, did little enquire after, or concern himself about the spiritual doctrine, Light, Love and Truth of Christ, but only about the government; and upon this only account of Christ's being against Caesar, and his own coveting to be accounted Caesar's friend, he sentenced him unto death. So here also in the Philosophical Work, Saturn, the dark astringent property, does not at all concern itself, with this or that internal loving quality of Venus, being not able to receive anything thereof into its own essence; but only for the pre-dominion is all this great contest. Saturn will not lose the friendship of Mars and Mercury, which both are with him in the same sphere, and jointly make up therein their own government, which needs must be overthrown, if Venus should be permitted to arise, and shine therein, with her Light and Love. And therefore he puts in execution that which is well pleasing unto them, and which they think may make for the preservation their wrathful government.

44. Pilate sent the Lord Christ unto Herod, and this mocked him, and put on him a long white garment. In this Philosophical Work, Herod the king answereth unto Sol, who is a king also in his own Principle. And this Sol puts upon Venus a simple, lunarish white colour; for it perceiveth that there lieth in Venus a solarish kingly power, and therefore it giveth unto her the white colour, from the Eternal liberty's Property, and would fain see, that she might open therein her powers from the Fire's centre, and show forth herself in a golden lustre (like as Herod would fain have seen a miracle wrought before him), which, if Venus did, she would be indeed a master and ruler over Mars and Mercury, but only in this outward world, a ruler in the Wrath, like as this Sol is also such a one. But as the Lord said unto Pilate, "My kingdom is not of this world", and would answer nothing unto Herod, nor his expectation by working any miracle before him; because in this white garment he stood only before the justice of God, and represented the poor, fallen Adam, in his false love of himself, whereof this white robe was an excellent and very significant figure, deeply by Behmen declared. So also in the Philosophical Work a breaking forth of the solarish power, in a golden lustre from the Fire's centre, and tincturing this white lunarish appearance of Venus, is all in vain expected; because the pure union, and universal tincture cannot be made manifest, except first all the dark Wrath and poison of Saturn, Mercury and Mars, be wholly drowned and swallowed up in blood and death.

45. Herod sent the Lord Christ back again to Pilate, and this, by his soldiers, stripped him, put on him a scarlet robe, scourged him, put upon his head a crown of thorns, and showed him to the multitude, which all cried out, "Crucify, crucify him", etc. So also in the Philosophical Work, Venus is delivered again unto Saturn, and he, with his strong, dark impression, lays hold on her, strips her of her fair robe, and puts on her a scarlet (purple) colour, wherein the Wrath of Mars is lodged. This colour (which will be adorned as with a glance or splendour in a flash), is from Saturn's and Mercury's Property, mixed with the fiery Mars, as the Artist shall distinctly see. When now the Lord Christ, in this royal robe, which was put upon him but in scorn and mockery, was presented to the Pharisees, Priests, and common people, they all cried out unanimously, "Away with him, he is but a false king, we own no other king but Caesar, etc." So also, when Venus in this royal colour, appears unto Mercury, Saturn and Mars and Luna also; this later being now changed in its will, joined herself with the three chief murdering Properties, and all together, with one consent, reject her, and as it were, cry out the very same; which is as much as to say, they dart forth their malignant, poisonous, fiery rays upon, and imprint the same into her, by the sharp impression of Saturn, so that the Artist shall see distinctly, that Venus is like as scourged and full of stripes. And moreover, which is indeed the greatest wonder, he shall exactly see the crown of thorns, with its sharp, stinging prickles, is put upon her. For as the whole process, in the suffering and death of Christ, is a circumstantial representation of all what the first Adam had acted in his transgression, in a quite contrary way, which is distinctly shown and declared by Behmen: And as the condition of Man in the Fall, is the same with the Earth's condition in the Curse, only different from it in degree, which he also not only answereth, but also demonstrateth sufficiently. So also the manner and process of their restoration, cannot but be alike in both. And as the Lord Christ in all his sufferings was most profoundly humble, and only passive, opening not his mouth but enduring all things most patiently, in a full submission to the pleasure of his Father: so also, in this Philosophical Work, the Artist shall see that Venus is wholly passive, standing all quiet and unmoveable, without any moving or stirring.

Many particulars more are by this author observed, and discoursed of, and this even so, that his discourse carried along with itself a plain and perceptible testimony of solidity. But for brevities sake they shall be but mentioned in short. The three nails wherewith Christ was nailed to the cross, are referred to the three first sharp, and piercing wrathful properties.

The two figures of the Virgin Mary and St. John, standing under the cross, are referred to the young man's and the virgin's life, now appearing in distinction, which the Artist (saith he) may see, if he hath eyes and understanding..

The words of Christ spoken on the Cross, "Father, forgive them, they know not what they do", are deeply and excellently declared. (1) as to the redemption of mankind, by showing, when Jesus destroyed death and selfhood in the humanity, he did not throw away that human property, wherein the Anger of God was kindled before, but even then he took it rightly and truly unto himself, that is, he took even then rightly the outward, out-spoken kingdom of wonders into the inward. And (2) As to this

Philosophical Work, by showing that the three murderers, when drowned in the lion's blood, do not pass away or are not annihilated, but they are forgiven, that is, their former hatred and wrathfulness, is turned into the highest Love-desire and they keep all their natural qualities, in their true order and office having lost nothing at all, but only their false and selfish predominion.

The two thieves, crucified with Christ, the one on the right hand, and the other on the left; the one mocking him, and the other turning unto him, and receiving the gracious promise "this day thou shalt be with me in Paradise"; are in this Philosophical Work referred to the kingdom of the Devil in the Wrath, and to the Kingdom of Love in the Light. Which two kingdoms are now separated the one from the other, etc. Thou shalt be with me in Paradise, says the Love, that is out of thy fiery, anguishing condition, thou shalt be turned and transmuted into me, etc. Here, saith Behmen, Venus in the Philosophical Work gets her Soul, for when Mars and Mercury die to the dark impression of Saturn, then Venus takes them in; then Anger and Love come to be one only being, Mars and Mercury become the Soul of Venus; all the strife ceaseth, the enmity is reconciled; Mercury is now all pure and hath no poison more in it, etc.

The words of Christ, saying to his mother, "Woman, behold thy son", and to St. John, "Behold thy mother", are excellently discoursed of by Behmen, not only with reference to the redemption of mankind, and to the universal Christian Church, but also to this Philosophical Work; wherein the Artist is to know, that he must imitate St. John, that all his work and operation is done only in or about the Mother, that is the kingdom of outward Nature, from which Christ here departeth; that his work in this world never will become totally and absolutely celestial, that he cannot manifest therein the Paradise, so as that God should appear therein face to face. But that he must abide all the time of this world, in the Mother only, though he verily obtaineth the universal Tincture in this Mother. Like as the mother of Christ also obtained it, in her being called by the angel, the Blessed among the women; notwithstanding, which she was afterwards to pass through temporal death, etc. So also the Artist obtaineth the blessing in this miserable world, so that he may tincture his corrupted earthly body, and preserve it in health, unto the terminus or end of his highest constellation, which is (N.B.) after or under Saturn. [When Saturn therefore is at his end and limit, and leaveth that life, which he hath been a leader of, no universal Tincture can prolong that life any longer.]

Concerning the words of Christ, "I thirst", and the vinegar mingled with gall, which when he had tasted, he would not drink, are profoundly declared -

(1) as an outward, most significant figure of what was transacted inwardly between the holy name Jesus, and the Anger of God awakened in the human soul. The name Jesus thirsted after the salvation of men, and would fain have tasted the pure living water in the human Property; but the Anger of God in the soul, gave itself into this thirsting Love-desire, which the Love would not drink, but yielded up itself, in a full resignation and obedience thereunto. Vinegar and gall are the proper figure of the human soul, viz., of these properties wherein the human soul essentially standeth, when considered as to its own proper being, without the Light. The soul, now here given again into the Holy Light's substantiality, which was in Adam, disappeared, etc. This caused such a two-fold great crack, as in the generation of Eternal Nature was explained. The first terrible crack made the Earth to quake, and rent the rocks asunder, etc. The second joyful crack raised the dead bodies of them that had

hoped and waited for the coming of the Messias, and rent also the vail in the temple, from the top to beneath, uniting now the human time with Eternity, etc.

(2) And as to the Philosophical Work, wherein Venus also thirsteth after the manifestation and pre-dominion of the Fire of love; but Mercury, in the sulphur of Mars and Saturn, presseth itself into her, with his killing Menstruum, which is the greatest poison, of the dark Wrathful source. But Venus, instead of drinking the same down, yieldeth up herself wholly thereunto, as if she did actually die. And from hence the great darkness in the Philosophical Work ariseth, so that the whole matter cometh to be so black as a raven.

When the inward sun of the Eternal Light's Principle, in the humanity, had given up itself into the dark Wrath and Anger of God, the outward sun in this third principle, which taketh all its glance and lustre from that Inward, as a representation, figure, or mirror thereof, could not shine. For if its root or deepest ground (considered as in the region of this world) was gone down into darkness, for to renew this principle into the Light, the outbirth of this root, that is the outward Sun, must needs have been darkened, contrary to the common course of Nature; And this even from the sixth hour of the day unto the ninth, which was the time of the first Adam's sleep, etc. In the Philosophical Work, as the Artist shall see, all what God hath done, in and with the humanity, when he was to redeem and bring it again into Paradise; so he shall see also in answerableness to this particular of the great supernatural darkness mentioned above, that when Venus thus yieldeth up her life, which all her glance and lustre dependeth upon, all her beauty must disappear, and darkness cometh up instead thereof. Nay, he shall see also, that not only Venus, in the three wrathful Properties, but also that these three themselves, in Venus, do lose their life altogether, and that all is now so black and dark as a coal. For here now life and death lie still and quiet together in the will of God, and to his only disposition. The whole is now reduced to the beginning, and standeth in that order, wherein it stood before the Creation. Nature's end is now attained unto, and all is fallen home unto, or into, the power of the first Fiat.

After this, the Lord cried out, "My God, why hast thou forsaken me?" The eternal, speaking Word stood now still, in the humanity, that is, it did not operate therein, so as to be sensibly felt thereby. For the heavenly humanity, which in Adam was disappeared, and in Christ quickened again, was to bruise the head of the Wrath, in the fiery soul, and to change the Soul's Fire into a clear, shining sun. That now this might be done, the humanity must be introduced into this Wrath, by the Eternal speaking Word, and by the same also, through this Wrath and death, into the solarish or paradisical life. When now this was done, the humanity could not but feel that Wrath in the soul, and in the same instant of this feeling, it could not feel the presence and power of the Eternal speaking Word, so as it could and did before, etc. And this was the forsaking.

So also in the Philosophical Work, when the wrathful properties swallow up the life of Venus, which is to change them into Sol, and to make that all seven may be one. Venus is forsaken. And this makes her lose her colour, and to be turned into Darkness, etc.

As the Lord Christ, after all his powerful works, miracles, overcoming of the Devil in the Temptation, and Transfiguration of his human body, was to go through all these sufferings, and at length wholly to die on the Cross, whereby he frustrated in a sense and manner, the hope and expectation of all his disciples. And as he had no other way or gate, than death, through which he could have entered into his glory, and drawn after him his members: So also in this Philosophical Work, the Artist hath hitherto seen indeed many wonderful things, and very glorious appearances, which made him to have a very great hope and expectation; yet for all this, now his expectation is in a sense quite overthrown and frustrated. For now the whole nature dieth in his work, and he must see that all is changed into a dark night. All the Properties, Powers, and Virtues, must now cease to be and do, what they were and did before, and must fall into the end of Nature. All yieldeth up its former life and activity, there is no more any stirring, moving, or operating. All the Properties are in the Crown-number, scattered in thousand, and so entered into the first Mysterium, in that state wherein they were before the Creation. The meaning is not that the outward materiality is made invisible, or quite annihilated, but only, that all the Powers therein which the outspoken Properties had from the Eternal speaking Word, and which were raised up against each other, in contrariety, each of them according to its own nature, are now at an end of their activity in self-will, and earthly inclination, and are fallen home again into the power of the Eternal speaking Word, having no other way, nor gate, but this death, through which they could enter from the curse into their primitive blessing. But when thus they are in death to themselves, and in the hand of the eternal Word, this cannot but raise them up again unto glory, as by a new Creation, and in answerableness the Resurrection of Christ.

The Lord Christ died indeed, as to the humanity from this world, but he took the same human body again in his Resurrection, and lost or left nothing thereof behind, but only the government of the four elements, wherein the Wrath, curse, and mortality lieth, etc. So in this Philosophical Work also, the first matter is not abolished or annihilated, but only the curse therein is destroyed, in the four elements, and the first life in the one Eternal Element is raised up again; and therefore it is now fix, and can abide the Fire. A glorious new body is now raised up out of the black darkness, in a fair white colour, but such a one as hath a hidden glance in it, so that the colour cannot be exactly discerned, until it resolveth itself, and the new Love-desire cometh up. And then in Saturn's centre, but in Jupiter's and Venus's Property, the Sun ariseth. This is in the Fiat, like as a new Creation, and when this is done, all the Properties cast forth unanimously their desire into Sol. And then the colour is turned into a mixture of white and red, from Fire and Light in union, that is, into yellow, which is the colour of majesty.

The appearance of love, to the wrathful properties of darkness, causeth, as mentioned above, a great crack, or terror. The wrathfulness is mightily exasperated by this appearance of Love, and presseth vehemently into her, for to swallow her up into death, which it doth also actually. But seeing that no death can be therein, the Love sinketh only down, yieldeth up herself into these murdering properties, and displayeth among them her own loving essentiality, which they must keep in them, and cannot get rid thereof. But even this is a poison unto death, and a pestilence unto Hell. For the wrathful Properties are also mightily terrified at this entering of Love into them, which is so strange and contrary to their own qualities, and which makes them all weak and impotent, so that they must lose their own will, strength, and pre-dominion, etc. So was it done in the death of Christ, and after such a manner (largely and excellently declared by Behmen). Death and curse in the humanity, was killed and destroyed, in and by the death of Christ, who, after his Resurrection, had no more the form of a male in his human body, but that of a paradisical Virgin, as Adam had before his fall. And so also is it, in this Philosophical Work. In this terror, crack, and mutual killing (though there is properly no death, but only a transmutation, or union of two into one), when Venus yieldeth up her life to the wrathful Properties, and when these, having lost their pre-dominion, are raised up again to a new life, the Virgin giveth her pearl to the young man, for a propriety. And so the life of the anger, and the life of the Love, are no more two, but only one; no more a male and female property, but a whole Virgin, with both tinctures united into one. When then the Artist seeth the red blood of the young man rise from death, and come forth out of the black darkness, together in union with the white colour of the virgin, he may then know that he hath the great Arcanum of the world, and such a treasure as is inestimable. Several things more could be brought forth from Behmen, which would afford many excellent considerations. But these may be sufficient, to show that harmonious analogy which is between the Restoration of fallen Man, through Jesus Christ, and the Restoration of cursed Nature, in the Philosophical Work.

www.ingramcontent.com/pod-product-compliance
Lightning Source LLC
LaVergne TN
LVHW041502070426
835507LV00009B/757